LAMBORGHINI

By Jennifer Colby

45TH PARALLEL PRESS

Published in the United States of America by Cherry Lake Publishing Group
Ann Arbor, Michigan
www.cherrylakepublishing.com

Reading Adviser: Beth Walker Gambro, MS Ed., Reading Consultant, Yorkville, IL
Book Designer: Jen Wahi

Photo Credits: © Tom B Paye/Shutterstock, cover, 1; © i viewfinder/Shutterstock, 4; © PhatTai/Shutterstock, 6; © Grisha Bruev/Shutterstock, 6; © Farabola/Alamy Stock Photo, 8; © Camerasandcoffee/Shutterstock, 12; © Oleksandr Grechin/Shutterstock, 13; © John Crowe / Alamy Stock Photo, 14; © Marton Szeles/Shutterstock, 16, 17; © Mau47/Shutterstock, 18, 20; © Johnnie Rik/Shutterstock, 19; © YES Market Media/Shutterstock, 21; © Glebiy/Shutterstock, 22, 24; © Artoholics/Shutterstock, 23; © classic topcar/Shutterstock, 27; © Mike Mareen/Shutterstock, 29; © S.Candide/Shutterstock, 30; © Jvelalo/Shutterstock, 30; © dan74/Alamy Stock Photo, 31.

45th Parallel Press is an imprint of Cherry Lake Publishing Group.

Library of Congress Cataloging-in-Publication Data

Names: Colby, Jennifer, 1971- author.
Title: Lamborghini / by Jennifer Colby.
Description: Ann Arbor, Michigan : Cherry Lake Publishing, [2022] | Series: Floored! Supercars
Identifiers: LCCN 2022005334 | ISBN 9781668909539 (hardcover) | ISBN 9781668911136 (paperback) | ISBN 9781668912720 (ebook) | ISBN 9781668914311 (pdf)
Subjects: LCSH: Lamborghini automobile--Juvenile literature. | Sports cars--Juvenile literature.
Classification: LCC TL215.L33 C635 2022 | DDC 629.222/2--dc23/eng/20220210
LC record available at https://lccn.loc.gov/2022005334

Printed in the United States of America by
Corporate Graphics

ABOUT THE AUTHOR:

Jennifer Colby is a school librarian in Ann Arbor, Michigan. She does not drive a supercar, but she likes going to auto shows to see what they look like.

Table of Contents

One place to see a Lamborghini supercar is at an auto show.

CHAPTER 1
What Are Supercars?

Cars get us where we need to go. We drive them to school and work. We drive them to the grocery store or a friend's house. If we need to go someplace, a car can get us there. But some car owners want a car that is more than a way to get from place to place. They want a car that is known for its high **performance**, **luxury**, or **technological** features. Performance is how well something works. Luxury means great comfort. Technological means using science and engineering. These car owners want to drive a **supercar**.

A supercar is a sports car. It is designed to provide a high-level driving experience. Drivers of supercars expect excellent **acceleration**, **handling**, and **maneuvering**. Acceleration is the act of moving faster. Handling is the way a car moves when it is driven. Maneuvering is a skillful way of moving.

Supercars are also known for their unique looks. You might see one of these eye-catching cars and admire it.

Have you seen a Lamborghini driving down the road? If so, then you have seen a supercar! What makes these cars so special?

Let's find out more about Lamborghinis.

With its upward-swinging doors and sleek body, a Lamborghini has a unique look.

The Lamborghini logo features a raging bull.

CHAPTER 2
Lamborghini History

The Lamborghini company began in Italy with founder Ferruccio Lamborghini. He was an excellent mechanic. He founded a tractor company in 1948. Lamborghini made his first tractors from old military car engines. In fact, the Lamborghini company still makes tractors today.

In 1963, Lamborghini created his car company in Bologna, Italy. With a focus on design, the company makes just a few models of cars. Today, they produce the Huracán, the Urus, and the Aventador.

Lamborghini was impressed by the strength of fighting bulls. He visited a Spanish bull ranch. After that visit, the raging bull became the logo for his new car company. The strength and speed of the bull represent a Lamborghini's performance.

Lamborghini liked fast cars. He owned many supercars. But his favorites were Ferraris—until their **clutches** broke. The clutch is the part of the car that allows it to switch gears. Lamborghini complained to carmaker Enzo Ferrari about the clutch issues. Ferrari replied, "The clutch is not the problem. The problem is you don't know how to drive a Ferrari and you break the clutch." Lamborghini decided to make cars that would drive the way he wanted them to.

In 1964, Lamborghini built the 350 GTV to be the perfect car. He wanted to make a car that performed well and was easy to drive. A smart businessman, he knew he could make more money selling sports cars than tractors. He even used some of the same parts from his tractors in his cars.

Lamborghini retired in 1974 at age 58. The Lamborghini brand is still known today for its high standards.

Ferruccio Lamborghini (right) explains the 350 GTV to a reporter.

The roomy design of the Urus is popular with many female car owners.

Behind the Wheel

Katia Bassi is the chief marketing officer at Lamborghini. She is in charge of promoting the brand. Since 2017, her goal has been to encourage more women to buy and drive Lamborghinis. She is the first woman to join the Lamborghini board of directors. These people make decisions about the company. When Bassi started, only 5 percent of Lamborghini owners were women.

In 2018, Lamborghini produced the Urus. It was the company's first true **SUV**. SUV stands for sport utility vehicle. Since the launch of the Urus, 11 percent of Lamborghini buyers have been women. Bassi believes that the Urus SUV appeals to women with its familiar and spacious SUV shape. It makes the transition to a supercar easier for them.

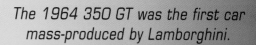

The 1964 350 GT was the first car mass-produced by Lamborghini.

CHAPTER 3

Lamborghini Evolution

The 350 GT was the first Lamborghini to be **mass-produced**. Mass-produced means to use machinery to produce large amounts of something. The 350 GT was very popular. Buyers liked its sleek design and powerful engine.

In 1966, Lamborghini introduced the Miura. It was the first supercar to have a **mid-engine layout**. A mid-engine layout puts the car's engine in front of the rear-wheel **axles** but behind the front axle. Axles are the metal rods that connect the wheels on either side of the car. This layout is now the standard for supercar designs.

For the next 10 years, Lamborghini continued to make high-performance cars. The scissor doors of the Countach rotate up from a hinge at the front of the door. With small rear windows, supercars are known for their poor visibility. Visibility means to be able to see. Scissor doors allow drivers to open the door to look out while they are backing up. No one said that supercars were practical. The Lamborghini scissor doors became so well known that they are called "Lambo doors."

The popular Countach was one of the first cars to have scissor doors.

HXI 5944

A Lamborghini Huracán GT3 EVO races along a closed track.

Over the years, people have raced Lamborghinis. Today, Lamborghinis race in two main events. They are the Super Trofeo and the Lamborghini GT3. The Super Trofeo is the longest-running single-carmaker racing championship in the world. It is a series of races on a closed track. Each privately funded team races the Huracán Super Trofeo EVO. More than 60 private Lamborghini racing teams participate in the GT3 championship. They drive the Huracán GT3 EVO on racetracks around the world.

The Lamborghini Huracán Super Trofeo EVO features a rear wing.

Lamborghinis race against other carmakers in the 24 Hours of Daytona (a 24-hour race) and the 12 Hours of Sebring (a 12-hour race). These **endurance races** take place in the United States. During endurance races, a team of drivers takes turns driving on a closed racetrack at high speeds over a long period of time. Lamborghinis have won the 12 Hours of Sebring 2 times.

A Lamborghini team has won the 24 Hours of Daytona 3 times.

The Sebring International Raceway in Sebring, Florida.

Lamborghinis and Ferraris are often compared to each other.

LAMBORGHINI VS. FERRARI

- Ferruccio Lamborghini started making cars when Enzo Ferrari told him to stick to making tractors.

- Lamborghinis are famous for their sharp lines, while Ferraris are known for their smooth ones.

- Lamborghini has only recently developed a racing team. Ferrari has won many Formula 1 races.

- Lamborghini's logo includes a raging bull. Ferrari's logo includes a rearing stallion.

- The fastest Lamborghini in production has a top speed of 217 miles (349 kilometers) per hour. It is 5 miles (8 km) per hour faster than Ferrari's fastest car.

Do you have a favorite Lamborghini?

Lamborghini Today

In 2020, Lamborghini introduced a **hybrid** car concept model called the Sián. A hybrid car is powered with a gasoline engine and an electric motor. With the addition of an electric engine, it is the carmaker's most powerful car. The Sián can go from 0 to 60 miles (97 km) per hour in less than 2.8 seconds. It would take an average car more than 8 seconds to do the same!

By 2024, the carmaker hopes to produce only hybrid cars. The Urus will be the first Lamborghini mass-produced model to have a hybrid engine.

Lamborghini's commitment to the environment does not stop with its cars. Their offices and car production site in Italy have been certified carbon neutral since 2015.

In 2021, Lamborghini was the first carmaker to give Amazon Alexa control of the car. Drivers of the Huracán EVO can adjust lighting, navigation, phone calls, and more with the "Alexa" voice command.

Lamborghinis cost a lot! The least expensive model is the Urus. It costs $218,009. One of the most expensive models in production is the Aventador SVJ Roadster. It costs $581,661. The expense of owning a Lamborghini does not stop at the purchase price. It also costs a lot of money to maintain a Lamborghini.

No matter how much it is driven, a Lamborghini requires annual service. This can cost up to $5,000! If the car is driven more than 7,500 miles (12,070 km) in a year, it will need new tires. The tires on a Lamborghini are made of a softer material that grips the road. A set of 4 new tires costs $2,000. A set of 4 new tires on an average car costs about $500.

Lamborghini sales were up for 2021.

Cost of Ownership

MODEL	PRICE
2021 Honda CRV	$25,350
2021 Ford Escape	$25,555
2021 Chevy Suburban	$52,300

MODEL	PRICE
2021 Lamborghini Urus	$218,009
2021 Lamborghini Huracán EVO	$261,275
2021 Lamborghini Huracán EVO Spyder	$293,695
2021 Lamborghini Aventador S	$425,021
2021 Lamborghini Aventador SVJ Roadster	$581,661
2021 Lamborghini Sián FKP 37	$2,640,000

Lamborghinis require service by an experienced technician. Lamborghini owners need to find someone who knows how to work on their car. This is not easy to do. There are only about 30 Lamborghini service centers in the United States!

Lamborghinis are known for their cutting-edge designs. Ferruccio Lamborghini's love of design and performance shows in today's models. For many people, a Lamborghini is like no other supercar!

For Lamborghini, new car design Terzo Millennio represents the future.

Timeline of a Legend

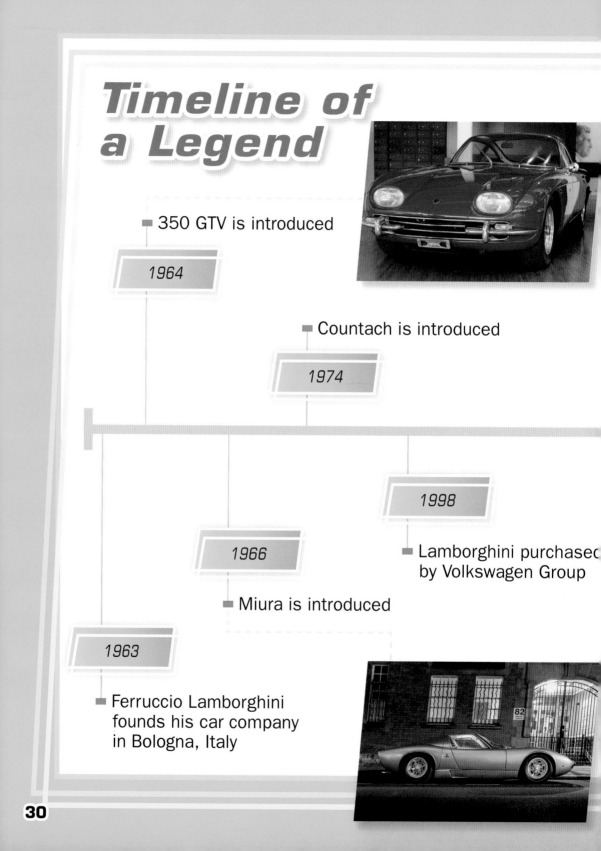

■ 350 GTV is introduced

1964

■ Countach is introduced

1974

1998

1966

■ Lamborghini purchased by Volkswagen Group

■ Miura is introduced

1963

■ Ferruccio Lamborghini founds his car company in Bologna, Italy

Lamborghini wins first 24 Hours
of Daytona endurance race

2018

Sián hybrid engine concept
car is introduced

2020

2018

Lamborghini wins first 12 Hours
of Sebring endurance race

2017

Terzo Millennio concept
car is introduced

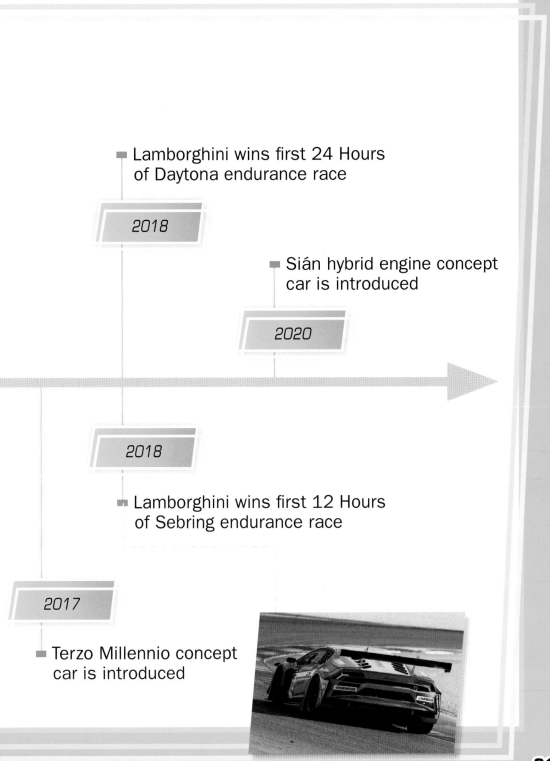

Find Out More

BOOKS

Garstecki, Julia. *Lamborghini Aventador*. North Mankato, MN: Black Rabbit Books, 2020.

Kingston, Seth. *The History of Lamborghinis*. New York, NY: PowerKids Press, 2019.

WEBSITES

Kiddle—Lamborghini Facts for Kids
https://kids.kiddle.co/Lamborghini

Lamborghini—History
https://www.lamborghini.com/en-en/history

Glossary

acceleration (ik-seh-luh-RAY-shuhn) the act of moving faster

axles (AK-suhlz) the metal rods that connect the wheels on either side of the car

clutches (CLUHCH-ez) parts of the car that allow it to switch gears

endurance races (in-DUHR-uhns RAY-suhz) closed-track races where a team of drivers takes turns driving at very high speeds over a long period of time

handling (HAND-ling) the way a car moves when it is driven

hybrid (HYE-bruhd) powered with a gasoline engine and an electric motor

luxury (LUHK-shuh-ree) great comfort and wealth

maneuvering (muh-NOO-vuh-ring) moving in a skillful way

mass-produced (MASS-pruh-DOOST) made in large amounts

mid-engine layout (mihd-EN-juhn LAY-owt) when the engine is in front of the rear-wheel axles and behind the front axle

performance (puh-FOHR-muhns) how well something functions or works

supercar (SOO-puhr-kar) sports car designed for a high-level driving experience

SUV (ESS YOO VEE) vehicle designed to be used on rough surfaces but often used on city roads

technological (tek-nuh-LAH-jih-kuhl) relating to science and engineering

visibility (vih-zuh-BIH-luh-tee) able to see

Index